BLOCKCHAIN 101

Fundamentals of a New Economy

MONIKA PROFFITT

BLOCKCHAIN 101
Fundamentals of a New Economy

ISBN-13: 978-1724928870
ISBN: 1724928872

I dedicate this book to Carol, without whom the last ten years would have never been possible.

CONTENTS

ACKNOWLEDGMENTS

This book is the brain child born from many illuminating conversations with many brilliant minds. The number of interesting and interested people that I have met in the blockchain space is astounding, Never before have I encountered so many people who genuinely want to help one another out and collaborate for the better good. The first of these bright, well intentioned souls is Robin Farmanfarmaian, my inspiring friend and professional mentor. From developing a signature look to knowing just what to say to a reporter, I have grown by leaps and bounds by simply observing this force of nature in her own (well tailored) habitat. I also have to give a shout out to the generous lawyers, entrepreneurs, and blockchain evangelists who have helped me find my way in the space when my lantern went out. Most notably, I'd like to thank the usual suspects on my last blockchain speaking tour, the likes of which could only have been dreamed up by a selection panel that values honesty, determination, and a well made piña colada. These delightful humans include Adryenn Ashley, John Kirk, Keller Fisher, and the eternally friendly Phil

Mrzyglocki. Y'all know how to bring the knowledge to the panel and the soul to the party. May New Orleans live on forever.

My gratitude extends to all of the women who have made it higher up than those who came before them, and who then made it a point to send the elevator back down. These are the women who have handed me a hammer when the glass ceiling teased me with a "no you can't." These include the doers of cool shit everywhere, to my high school guidance counselor who, many years ago, went so far as to forge a much needed signature to get me out of high school and on to the next project. What a relief.

I want to thank Tim Draper for challenging me about my use of the term "social impact" and questioning a business that identifies with such lofty and (to some) irrelevant notions. Thank you thank you thank you. I made a name for myself that night, simply by holding my own in our impassioned debate. On a related note, I'd like to also thank my own off the cuff strategy of intentional ignorance when it came to you, Tim. Due to the fact that I didn't know which judge on the panel was The Billionaire, I didn't know who was giving me a hard time. Because of this, I didn't get tripped up by being deferential to the dude who was, arguably, a really big deal. Go strategic ignorance!

I'd like to thank my late father, Micheal Proffitt, for reiterating to me that I needed to learn to be a number, to get along as a member of the crowd, and not to take up too much space or ask for anything special. Like with many insights imparted to children, that perspective provided me the fuel to go out on my own young, in a wholly unique direction, and bring my own signature to every twist and turn my life has taken since, never fitting in and never really trying to.

I'd like to thank my mother and step-father, Claire Sheridan and Kelsey Kennedy, without whom I might have put away my ideas about securitization, real estate, and the power of the crowd. After countless hours on zoom calls, spreadsheets littering our desks, a sizable bite has been taken out of solving some major issues regarding tools for wealth redistribution and alternatives to the current lending system. In particular, Kelsey's patience over the last couple of years has convinced me he is up for admission amongst the apostles. For a couple of septenarians, you two have done a splendid job of keeping an open mind about this whole un-backed, digital money stuff. You are so much cooler than you let on.

Finally, and most earnestly, I'd like to thank Austin Kennedy, a true blockchain expert and my favorite behind the scenes social media magician. Your help with my dizzying array of projects, and with this book in particular, has been herculean. I am eternally grateful for your fierce work ethic and insightful commentary on everything from public opinion to technical specs. Your mind is a marvel and I can't wait to see the incredible heights that you reach in the years to come.

INTRODUCTION

"The first generation of the digital revolution brought us the internet of information. The second generation — powered by blockchain technology — is bringing us the internet of value."

- Don Tapscott

Last Thanksgiving, my cousin, who lives in Houston, Texas and works in the Gulf of Mexico on oil and gas rigs, asked me to explain to him "this blockchain stuff you're doing". Of course, being a metaphor-loving, free-associating type of thinker, I rattled off an analogy. I told him to imagine a blockchain as a game of telephone. A word is fed to the first person (a node), who must pass the word to the next person (another node). The only way for the game to be won is if the last person receives the exact same word as the first, meaning that every person (node) in between agreed on the word. If they do not come up with the same word at the end of the round, they must start over until they get it right. In this special game of telephone, once a round is won, the resulting information is entombed in bulletproof glass to be viewed publicly for eternity.

Except the whole point of telephone is that it never goes that way. He looked at me with a blank stare, as if to say, really, this is what your life has become? A game of telephone? So I tried again, because no, *that's not what my life has become*. But this time, the analogy unfortunately ended up putting his wife's Instagram feed on questionable footing in the delicate balance between good and evil in social media. I told him that all information on a blockchain database is verified by many different people and stored forever in an unchangeable archive. So, think of it kind of like Instagram, except without the delete feature, where no posts could ever be taken down, and all were immediately still seen by everyone who is following her. Like, all of our family. Any impulsive selfie would live eternally in the chronological "chain" of information.

His eyes narrowed and he coolly informed me that I was "adding to the problem."

But all weak metaphors and jokes aside, this is a very, very exciting time in technology and the kind of widely available, secure access that it is about to provide. This is not just access to a platform that allows you to embarrass your husband, or let the world know your latest haiku. This is the most important thing to happen to our communication, to money, and to virtually every industry, since the mass adoption of internet itself.

Those of us who are "in the know" are beating our drums and making as much noise as possible to get your attention.

I predict that we are on the cusp of an economic revolution, and those of us who understand what this means for the future of money, value, and economic mobility, are going to be best equipped to take advantage of the new prospects that are created. Those of us who are "in the know" are beating our drums and making as much noise as possible to get your attention. Because unlike when the internet first arrived, a tool we all now use on a daily, or more likely, hourly basis, Blockchain (yes, it gets capitalized this time) is a technology that is made for a revolution. It was designed for the masses. In fact, it only works properly with mass adoption, and the broader and more diverse the user base, the more secure and accurate it is.

As you can see, I have strong feelings for this new invention, so you can also rest assured that I will do my best to explain the basics of blockchain so that you can become a part of it, too. To do this, I want to give you the easiest way to understand blockchain technology and get familiar with what all of this crypto-Bitcoin-Ethereum excitement is about. Because the train is coming, and we all need to get on it for us to get anywhere. That's the unique thing about blockchain, it is made for broad participation, and without that, it actually doesn't accomplish what it was made to do as a distributed ledger. Many people speculate that we are experiencing the equivalent of the 90s once again, in terms of technological revolution. When they dig deeper, often blockchain enthusiasts and speculators posit, are we in 1995 or 1999? Meaning, is this going to be a bubble or is this here to stay? Is it about to burst or is it just getting going? And let's face it, with the internet's arrival, and the flurry of activity, innovations, bad ideas, great ideas, and, eventually, mass adoption, it is both. The 1990s held a technological bubble in one hand, and a revolution in the other, just like now.

That's the exciting part.

In this simple guide, my aim is to quickly bring you from zero to confident, so that you fully understand the buzzwords that keep popping up - terms like Bitcoin (what is it exactly, and why should I care about it?), blockchain (sounds oppressive, frankly), and crypto (crypt... is it dead?). All of this is a part of the digital landscape of money, and there are several hills and valleys that you need to know about in order to traverse it.

To know our way around, we'll delve into digitally enforced smart contracts, cryptocurrencies, and distributed ledgers, which are just some of the exciting technologies that are set to fundamentally change the global economy. You will see that as these technologies grow in user adoption, people will ultimately allow everyday investors real-time access to entirely new asset classes available only through blockchains technology - and along with that, users (meaning you) will be able to reap the financial benefits in ways that many of us never dreamed of before.

01

THE BLOCKCHAIN DICTIONARY

"You can't stop things like Bitcoin. It will be everywhere and the world will have to readjust. World governments will have to readjust."

- John McAfee

THE BLOCKCHAIN DICTIONARY

To learn the basics of the blockchain space, the best place to begin is with understanding the terms that are commonly used. The easiest way to shut down a curious listener or possible adopter of a new paradigm is to throw around words that are in essence foreign and unintuitive, so before we dive into concepts of blockchain or any examples of use cases, let's start with the fundamental building blocks, the key terms.

In addition to providing simple, easy to understand definitions of commonly used terms, there are also going to be many analogies that will provide context for these new, decentralized functions that blockchain is known for.

BITCOIN

Bitcoin is a peer-to-peer digital currency that was invented by an unknown person or group of people under the pseudonym Satoshi Nakamoto and released as open-source software in 2009. Bitcoin is a mathematical solution to the "double-spend" dilemma. New Bitcoins are minted through a process called "mining," in which participants are rewarded fractions of Bitcoin for validating the network data.

Imagine a series of indestructible glass mailboxes connected by an underground network of tunnels. The mailboxes cannot be opened by anything except for their unique individual keys. Even when they are opened, the contents cannot be taken out—only sent elsewhere through the underground tunnel. The mailboxes' purpose is to store and transfer gold. If anyone knows your mailbox address, they can send you gold, and vice versa. Because the mailboxes are glass, anyone can see how much gold is inside of any mailbox at any time. However, anyone can get as many mailboxes as they want, so there is no way to know how many mailboxes everyone owns. Because the gold never physically leaves the mailbox network, and can only be transferred from mailbox to mailbox, there is no possibility of any gold being added or removed from the system. This is Bitcoin.

BITCOIN MINING

Bitcoin mining is the process by which transactions are verified and added to the public ledger, known as the blockchain. "Miners" dedicate their computer power to solving intricate mathematical problems on the blockchain and forming a consensus of information with other miners. Each validated "block" of information comes with a 12.5 BTC reward, which is split between the miners who validated the block.

The term mining is actually a pretty fitting one, even though there are no picks and no black lung diagnoses involved. For this example, imagine 100 miners hacking away at a magical ore. The magic ore releases a steady 12.5 ounces of gold every 10 minutes and that gold is distributed evenly amongst everyone who mined during the 10- minute period. Each miner receives 0.125 ounces of gold every 10 minutes. Now imagine 900 other miners hear about the profits, so they show up at the magic ore. The ore continues to release 12.5 ounces of gold every 10 minutes, but now each miner only receives 0.0125 ounces. Some of the original miners aren't making enough money to cover the costs of their expensive pickaxes and headlamps anymore, so they quit, forfeiting their future shares. This is Bitcoin Mining. Oh, and the magic ore's rewards are cut in half every four years.

BLOCKCHAIN

Blockchain is a digital ledger in which data is verified by a distributed network. In order for information to be recorded onto a blockchain, every network validator must agree on the information's legitimacy through a consensus protocol. When properly distributed, the ledger is immutable and unhackable.

Imagine you want to let your classmate, Cindy, borrow your pencil. How do you know she won't keep it? You'd better have the teacher watch the transfer happen so she can verify that the pencil really came from you. Oh, but Cindy is the teacher's pet. How can you be sure the teacher won't side with her if there is a dispute? You'd better have the whole class witness the transfer and agree that it is, in fact, your pencil before you hand it over. This is a blockchain.

CRYPTOCURRENCY

A cryptocurrency is a digital currency in which cryptographic techniques are used to regulate the generation of units of currency and verify the transfer of funds, often operating independently of a central bank or authority.

Imagine trying to throw a dollar bill from Texas to Singapore. It's a tall task, and even if it were possible, it would take a quite a long time to get there. What if that dollar bill were digital, not physical, and could be sent as easily and quickly as an e-mail? This is a cryptocurrency.

DISTRIBUTED LEDGER TECHNOLOGY (DLT)

Blockchains are dynamic distributed ledgers, meaning that every network participant holds a real-time copy of the data. Distributed Ledger Technology is a digital system for recording the transfer of assets in which the transactions and their details are recorded in multiple places at the same time. Unlike traditional databases, distributed ledgers have no central data storage or administration functionality.

ETHER (THE CURRENCY)

Ether is the primary cryptocurrency that exists within the Ethereum ecosystem. Ether can be transferred between accounts and is used to compensate miners on the Ethereum network for computations performed. Mistakenly, Ether (the currency) is often referred to as Ethereum (the network).

So you have a highway, and you are using it to get to all kinds of places, but this highway needs perpetual maintenance. So some people (cryptocurrency miners) work on the highway, keeping it smooth and in good condition, all of the time. In return they are rewarded with Ether, which is like a highway currency, or a toll coin. You can also just buy toll coins, and it turns out that as more and more people use the high-way, the value of the toll coins goes up and down, depending on the traffic and the belief that people have in the highway system as a whole.

ETHEREUM (THE NETWORK)

Ethereum is an open-source, blockchain-based distributed computing platform which supports smart contracts. Transactions on the Ethereum network are fast and inexpensive.

Imagine soccer balls in an arena. The arena has a force field that prevents the soccer balls from ever leaving. People can come into the arena and kick the balls around. They can play games with the balls, invent new games, and even start soccer ball businesses inside the arena. The more players and entrepreneurs that come into the arena and want to use the balls, the more value the soccer balls hold. The soccer balls are Ether, and the arena which facilitates the many uses of soccer balls is Ethereum.

EXCHANGE

An exchange is a digital marketplace where traders can buy and sell different cryptocurrencies and assets. Centralized exchanges are the most common, and they are the kind of exchange which is hosted by a central company. The central company is responsible for maintaining the marketplace and securing the funds deposited into the marketplace. Decentralized exchanges are less common, but far more secure. In a decentralized exchange, all exchanges are made by smart contracts and require no involvement by a central authority. Funds are exchanged from wallet to wallet.

Imagine a bazaar owned by a King where peasants can trade gold, salt, and other forms of currency. Each trade incurs a small tax for the King. This is a centralized cryptocurrency exchange. Now imagine the peasants create a bazaar where they never need to leave their houses, and the King does not know of any transactions they make. To initiate a trade, peasants send requests through pigeons, and pigeons transfer the gold, salt, etc. from door to door. This is a decentralized exchange.

FIAT MONEY

Paper money or coins of little or no intrinsic value in themselves and not convertible into gold or silver, but made legal tender by order of the government. Fiat money is often stable in value day-to-day, though inflationary over time.

Imagine a currency owned by a government, with no known supply, and no limit to the supply that can be created. Oh, wait, you already have it in your bank account. The use of the term "fiat" in the cryptocurrency world is a not so sly way of underscoring the fact that, even though the big criticism of cryptocurrencies is that they are not backed by anything (even though some of them, most notably security coins, are). When you call the US Dollar a fiat currency, you are recognizing what has been the case for decades, that the US Dollar is not backed by gold anymore. It is not backed by anything, but it has a value because many, many people use it and accept it and believe in it. Not because they can trade it in for gold at any point (they can't, not anymore), but because there is a massive adoption of it as a usable, tradable currency. It doesn't need to be backed by anything, it is backed, in essence, by belief. Cheeky (and accurate) of the crypto world to call that out.

HODL

HODL is an enthusiastic misspelling of the word "hold" which originated from a Bitcoin forum post in December 2013. It has since become a common vocabulary word in the cryptocurrency community. It is used most often to describe the act of keeping a currency for the long term (holding it) instead of selling it.

"Don't sell that while it's down, Jimmy! You only lose when you sell. HODL it!"

You might have seen HODL on a t-shirt or in one of your social media feeds and been confused at the time. It is clearly misspelled, and it is supposed to be spelled HOLD, but people are silly, and they say and repeat slightly absurd things all the time. That is all.

INITIAL COIN OFFERING (ICO)

An ICO is a fundraising mechanism in which startup companies sell their tokens in exchange for Bitcoin, Ether, or other money. It is comparable to an Initial Public Offering (IPO), though not yet regulated by the Securities and Exchange Commission.

Imagine a man strolls into a village on his horse and reserves a spot in the village green for one month. He stands in his spot each day, announcing a plan to start a farm and grow mung beans. He tells about the wondrous benefits of mung beans and their promising medicinal potential. He lets the village people know that mung beans have yet to be discovered by the masses and that they can be among of the first to own some—if they will only help him fund his farm. He offers mung beans from a limited supply at a rate of 10 beans per ounce of gold. The village people buy up the mung beans with all the gold they have, and by the end of his first week, the man is all out of beans to sell. He rides off into the night, promising to return when the farm is built. The village people, once inspired and amazed, are now left without their gold, wondering "Will the man ever come back? Are mung beans really the future of medicine?" This is an example of how an ICO can be a scam. When the mung bean farm is built and profitable, the people of that village have encountered great fortune that only kings before them could have participated in funding.

SECURITIES EXCHANGE COMMISSION (SEC)

The SEC is a U.S. government agency that oversees securities transactions, activities of financial professionals and mutual fund trading to prevent fraud and intentional deception. The SEC consists of five commissioners who serve staggered five-year terms.

(See example from ICO) Imagine there were a group of trusted men who verified the legitimacy of the mung bean business and insured all of the gold that the village people invested. This is the SEC. Oh, and they also make sure the village people pay taxes on any gains they make from their mung bean investments.

SMART CONTRACT

A smart contract is a function that is carried out autonomously by a computer. Smart contracts allow the reliable performance of predetermined functions and transactions without the need for third parties or human interaction.

Imagine a spell is placed on a man to do everything exactly as he was told to do it and be completely outright about everything he does. He could be an intermediary of trade, he could facilitate votes, he could referee sports. There would never be a dispute about his actions because he does everything exactly as he was instructed to, and he is always honest about his intentions. The only mistakes he could ever possibly make are mistakes in the instructions he is given. This is a smart contract.

TOKEN (NOT A COIN)

A token represents a particular fungible and tradable asset with utility. Tokens are often the core assets of blockchain ecosystems which are used to carry out smart contracts and other functionalities. A *coin*, though similar in nature, does not have utility and is simply used as a means of payment.

Imagine you go into Chuck-E-Cheese and exchange your US dollars for some gold tokens to play the various games. While you're at Chuck-E-Cheese, these coins have endless possibilities. You can play games, earn prize tickets, and maybe even purchase some snacks with them. They have value. Now leave Chuck-E-Cheese. Can you buy games with them? Can you buy food with them? Can you take these tokens to Six Flags? The answer in all three cases is no. As it turns out, unless they are listed on an exchange to be traded for other tokens, they only hold value within the ecosystem they were made for. This is a token. Also known as computer money, if you're talking to your inner five year old.

TOKENOMICS

Tokenomics refers to the economics of a token, or the economic rules that have been set to give a token value. A token's supply, initial value, and allocation, are examples of tokenomics.

WALLET

A cryptocurrency wallet is a client-side interface which stores the public and private keys used to receive or spend a cryptocurrency. They offer attractive and non-intimidating ways of interfacing with a blockchain, and though cryptocurrencies are never actually deposited *into* a wallet client, they offer the appearance of a real-life wallet in which funds are stored.

02 BITCOIN VS. CRYPTO VS. BLOCKCHAIN

"The blockchain symbolizes a shift in power from the centers to the edges of the networks."

-**William Mougayar**

LET'S START WITH THE CURRENCY...

To begin, Bitcoin is a digital currency or cryptocurrency, that can be used in digital transactions that don't have to involve a bank or third party. Bitcoin goes up and down in price according to people's belief of what it is worth, and therefore, crowd's desire to buy or sell it.

THE DIGITAL LANDSCAPE OF MONEY...

Crypto refers to the world of cryptocurrencies, or digital currencies, that have been created and are in some state of being created, used, traded, bought, sold, held, and/or mined. Bitcoin is a crypto, but crypto is bigger than bitcoin. Bitcoin is but a tree in the forest of crypto. But a very tall and well-known tree, and one that, if it fell, would definitely be heard.

Bitcoin is a crypto, but crypto is bigger than bitcoin.

THE GLOBE UPON WHICH IT SITS...

Blockchain is the earth itself that this forest grows upon. Like I mentioned before, it is like Instagram without the delete feature for data and digital money. It is the technology that enables all of these currencies to be created and traded. It is also the bedrock that allows the information related to these currencies to be incorruptible and known without the need for a central authority for verification.

PUBLIC VS. PRIVATE BLOCKCHAINS: THE PROS AND CONS

Blockchains were originally conceived for the purpose of circumventing centralization. The inventor, Satoshi Nakamoto, wanted to cut intermediaries out of payment systems and make a pure peer-to-peer system that would be validated by participants across the world. Recently, however, with the excitement around the new technology in the media, businesses have begun to explore the idea of a privatized blockchain, which we'll get to shortly.

WHAT IS A PUBLIC BLOCKCHAIN?

A public or "open" blockchain is a transparent record of transactions that can be confirmed by anyone who cares to participate in the network. There is no requirement to meet conditions for admission into the network. Anyone with a computer and internet access is able to participate in all functions of the system.

The classic example of a public blockchain is the Bitcoin network. Anyone who wants to participate can create a Bitcoin wallet, purchase Bitcoin and begin transacting on the network. Anyone can become a miner, or validator, by dedicating their computer's resources to mining pools. In return, they will receive a small income generated by fees and block rewards.

PROS OF A PUBLIC BLOCKCHAIN

• Since the hashing power is distributed and there are no 'trusted third parties' involved in the validation process, public blockchains are incredibly secure. Since Bitcoin's inception in 2008, the blockchain has not been hacked, edited, or reversed. The more miners a network has, the more impossible it becomes to produce the majority of the hashing rate, and so no single entity ever controls the information. This is what makes blockchain technology so valuable.

• Public blockchains are trustless systems, meaning that there is no trust involved in the consensus mechanisms. If something is recorded onto the blockchain, participants can be sure that the network agreed on the event's legitimacy and so that event is accurate.

• There are no points of failure in this system. Even if the largest mining company in the world, Bitmain, were to shut down all of its miners and nodes, the network wouldn't flinch. There are nodes throughout the world, in nearly every country, that would pick up the slack.

• The integrity of public blockchains is unmatched. Anyone who participates in the network can be sure that their actions will be carried out exactly as the protocol commands it to.

CONS OF A PUBLIC BLOCKCHAIN

- The cost per transaction in a public blockchain can be high since the validators of the network expect a reward for their contributions. For example, when someone sends a Bitcoin, they are charged a transaction fee which is used to pay the miners who validated the block. The miners must make enough money to cover the costs of their work, including electricity, internet, and hardware costs, which can be quite expensive. The fees are variable and the more demand is put on miners, the higher the fees rise.

- The transactions added to the blockchain are open for anyone in the world to view. Because of this, they are not ideal for recording sensitive information.

- Since public blockchains must create a consensus between all of the nodes within the system, a lot of redundancy is involved and a massive amount of computational power is required. Bitcoin has been called a threat to the environment for this very reason.

WHAT IS A PRIVATE BLOCKCHAIN?

In contrast with the original public blockchains, private blockchains are permission-based systems. This means that, unlike the Bitcoin network which can be accessed by anyone with a computer, private blockchains require an invitation for participation. Because of this, the network validation is done solely by either the network creator or by a set of rules written by the network creator. The mining capabilities and the consensus algorithm are completely centralized within the palms of the creator.

In a blockchain that is private, each user does not have equal rights within it. Users are granted permissions to access certain types of data and complete specific functions. Everything else remains closed. The mechanism of access depends on the rules set forth by the network creator. Existing participants could grant access to future entrants, a single authority could grant licenses, or an organization within the ecosystem could make the decisions.

In a blockchain that is private, each user does not have equal rights within it.

The same mechanisms can be used to determine the roles of individual participants within the network.

One of the most well-known private chains is IBM's Hyperledger Fabric. Hyperledger Fabric is an information queuing system with modified partitions. The partitions act as a sequence of messages that are continuously connected with one another, creating a sort of 'chain.' There are no traditional 'blocks,' or groups of data that are verified every few seconds. Instead, the entire sequence of transactions is processed in a single queue at the end of each day. This system is validated by a group of 'nodes' owned by IBM, making the system technically 'decentralized,' but since the nodes are all owned by the same entity, the power within the network is central.

PROS OF A PRIVATE BLOCKCHAIN

- In a private blockchain, the validation is carried out by the network creator and therefore no miners are hoping to profit on network facilitation. As a result, there are very low fees or no fees at all.

- When a consensus mechanism is centralized, it is much faster, and unnecessary altogether. The network nodes do not need to agree with each other when they are all owned by the same entity. Instead of waiting for a network consensus, information can be recorded immediately (sounding no different from a traditional database, right?).

- The owner of the network can control who is able to record information and to whom the recorded information is visible.

CONS OF A PRIVATE BLOCKCHAIN

- The blockchain can be manipulated since it is centralized. The 51% attack, mentioned earlier, illustrates this exact issue. When someone owns the majority hashing power of a blockchain network, they can rewrite the data within it, and therefore the information is not immutable or secure.

- Blockchains are far more complicated and expensive to maintain than a traditional database.

- In order to run a blockchain, a business needs to employ distributed validation nodes that will constantly validate data, incurring electricity and hardware costs along the way.

- There is always a point of failure in a centralized system. If the company maintaining the blockchain loses power, the blockchain shuts down.

SOME FOOD FOR THOUGHT

Because many corporations are not fully apprised of what blockchain technology really is and where its value lies, IBM and other early blockchain promoters can profit from the misleading media hype by offering "innovative" blockchain solutions for businesses., that actually aren't innovative at all. IBM charges up to $120,000 per year for the hosting of their Hyperledger Fabric system, and in many cases, this only serves to complicate existing databases (which already work completely fine, by the way). Companies hoping to be on the cutting edge of the new blockchain-driven economy will hop on this idea and implement block-chain solutions, though they will quickly realize that these solutions add a lot of complications and ex-penses, and might have been fine if they had been left alone, in a pre-blockchain state.

Designed to keep public out and introducing "trusted" middlemen, private blockchains forget that trusted third parties are actually security holes.

Iryo Network, a distributed healthcare project, ex-plained the issues of a private blockchain in a blog post:

"Contrary to popular belief, aided by deceptive blockchain marketing, blockchains are not a good solution for storing data. Each piece of information that you store in the blockchain sits in hundreds or more nodes (more than 100,000 in the case of Bitcoin) making it an extremely costly solution. This is why the Iryo Network doesn't store data on blockchain but instead, uses blockchain to ensure the transparency of transactions.

At Iryo, we consider databases and blockchains that are not opened to the public to be insecure. They can easily be altered by the business running them at their discretion, and they go against the ethos of the open and transparent cryptocurrency space. Designed to keep public out and introducing "trusted" middlemen, private blockchains forget that trusted third parties are actually security holes."

03

COINS AND
THEIR
FUNCTIONS

"Blockchain technology isn't just a more efficient way to settle securities. It will fundamentally change market structures, and maybe even the architecture of the internet itself."

- **Abigail Johnson**

A ROSE BY ANY OTHER NAME

There are several different types of coin and tokens, and by that, I mean there's a variety of different behaviors that different cryptocurrencies resemble. This is because the people making these currencies are literally writing the rules for how they work. Sound confusing? It can be, and for this reason, I am going to drill into the main types of currencies that are currently on the market.

SECURITY (EQUITY) TOKENS

Security tokens are tokens that act as stocks or shares in a company or asset. Often these coins employ Proof-of-Stake systems (PoS), in which token holders are rewarded periodically for "staking" (holding) their tokens—similar to dividends paid by public corporations to shareholders. These tokens are beginning to be recognized by the U.S. Securities and Exchange Commission (SEC) as securities, and so these tokens are subject to the same taxes and regulations as typical corporate shares—making them the most traditional class of tokens in the cryptocurrency market.

SECURITY TOKEN USES

Security tokens are used for common investment purposes. They are typically offered in the form of an "Initial Coin Offering," or ICO, which is similar to an Initial Public Offering, or IPO. Investors purchase tokens from a company in hopes that their coins will gain value and accrue dividends as the company grows.

PAYMENT COINS

Payment coins are treated by the SEC as a commodity. This is because they do not offer dividends to holders, and they are solely used for the purpose of transferring and storing wealth. A classic example of a payment coin is Bitcoin. While Bitcoin and its core technology are constantly being amended and improved, value increases of Bitcoin are largely a result of supply and demand. Because its value is not tied directly to the success of an underlying company, and does not offer a dividend, the SEC has equated Bitcoin to other commodities such as gold.

PAYMENT COIN USES

Payment coins are primarily used in place of money. They can be used to make purchases, pay wages, and store value.

UTILITY TOKENS

Utility tokens are tokens that are purchased to be applied toward a specific function. They are not designed for investment purposes, and so they are not treated as securities by regulatory watchdogs. Instead, utility tokens are equated to in-app tokens or digital coupons which are used to buy virtual goods and services.

Tom Emmer of the SEC commented:

"We certainly can imagine a token where the holder is buying it for its utility and not as an investment, and in those cases, especially if it's a decentralized network in which it's used, and there are no central actors who have information asymmetries or where they would know more than token investors."

UTILITY TOKEN USES

Utility tokens can be used for a variety of purposes. The use cases are only limited by the imagination of the creators. Typically, they will offer users access to specific services. For example, buying utility tokens before their price is driven up by supply and demand will effectively grant holders a discount on said services.

CIRCULATION

Supply and demand affect all three of these classes of tokens, so circulation plays an important in determining their value. If there is too large of a circulating supply, it may doom the coin to an eternity of low value, while too low of a supply may prevent a coin from ever being adopted by the masses.

Supply and demand affect all three classes of tokens, so circulation plays an important in determining their value.

Consider this scenario from my last trip abroad, where I found myself late to catch a flight in Bangkok. I was in a cab on my way to the airport, and I had run out of the local currency, the Thai baht. The cab driver didn't take credit cards, but I did have some US dollars on me, so I asked if I could pay with USD instead. He gladly accepted. Why? Because he knew how widely circulated US dollars are—and he recognized their value.

People will accept USD, knowing that it can be easily converted to other currencies or used to pay for goods and services. Had I offered him Zimbabwean Blind Note or a Mexican Peso, he would likely not have felt confident enough to accept it since those currencies are not well circulated, and therefore they do not have far-reaching liquidity or recognizable value.

04

SECURITY AND THEFT

---

*"The blockchain does one thing: it replaces third-party trust with mathematical proof
that something happened."'*

- Adam Draper

SECURITY HOLES

If blockchains are so secure, why do I keep hearing about people hacked?

If you keep up with cryptocurrency news, you have certainly heard about the cyber theft running rampant in the industry. According to CNBC, the total amount of stolen cryptocurrencies in just the first half of 2018 was $1.1 billion. With blockchains being touted as impenetrable networks, you may be wondering how it is possible for so much crypto to get swiped.

The simple answer is that the majority of thefts have nothing to do with vulnerabilities in the blockchains themselves, but can instead be attributed to human error. With the traditional banking system, we rely heavily on the tools employed by our banks and governments to keep our money secure, and often times, we can't even see that these security systems are there.

With cryptocurrencies, there is no FDIC, no federal insurance that will make sure you are covered if the something with the technology goes wrong. Instead, you have the burden - and the freedom - of acting as your own bank. With crypto, you are solely responsible for the safety and security of your funds and without proper education on the subject, it can be quite easy to lose your digital coins. To make matters worse, cryptocurrency holders do not have legislative support to cover their losses in the case of a hack, so there is often no hope of recovering stolen funds.

In this section, we'll cover the various types of cyber theft and how you can avoid falling victim to them.

WALLET VULNERABILITIES

One of the first steps to keeping cryptocurrencies safe is finding the right wallet to store them in. There are two main types of wallets: hot wallets and cold wallets. Hot wallets are digital purses that are connected to the internet. By nature, hot wallets are not secure as they are open to incoming network connections. The safety of funds in a hot wallet is only as good as the security habits of the individual or third-party controlling the wallet.

A common form of hot wallet is an exchange wallet. To allow ceaseless trading between users across the globe, exchange wallets need to remain connected to the internet at all times. This susceptibility, combined with the volume of funds they hold makes exchange wallets a prime target for hackers.

Cold wallets are digital purses that are not connected to the internet, making them a much safer option. The most common form of cold wallet is a paper wallet. A paper wallet is a printed piece of paper that holds the private keys to a certain wallet address, usually in the form of a QR code. Until that private key is scanned and brought online, it remains completely shut off from all incoming network connections and therefore cannot be stolen.

Most crypto holders have both hot wallets and cold wallets. They keep small amounts of funds in the hot wallets to use for daily transactions, similar to a checking account, and they keep large sums in cold wallets for long-term storage, similar to a savings account.

It is important to note that exchange wallets are not the only form of hot wallet, and even desktop software wallets such as Exodus are able to be compromised. With desktop software wallets, the user is in control of their own private keys, but the wallet still lives on a computer and remains susceptible to any malware or virus that is downloaded and installed onto the host.

PHISHING AND SCAMS

The most prevalent (and successful) forms of cyber theft are fraudulent operations which trick crypto holders into handing over their funds, or worse, the keys to their wallets.

Phishing attacks are clever ways of disguising malicious sites as familiar, legitimate services in order to steal passwords, private keys, and eventually, money. New phishing attacks are invented every year, but one of the oldest and time-tested methods is the slight misspelling of URLs.

For example, to steal the passwords of Binance users, a scammer might put up an exact copy of the site, or a "mirror," under the URL www.bínance.com, with the "í" replaced by an "í" with an accent. The URL address looks similar enough to the real www.binance.com address that an unsuspecting victim would log in without giving it a second glance, effectively handing over their passwords to the thieves.

To avoid falling victim to password-snatching, it's important to bookmark your favorite exchanges or always type the web addresses manually to be sure that you end up on the correct sites.

To avoid falling victim to password-snatching, it's important to bookmark your favorite exchanges or always type the web addresses manually to be sure that you end up on the correct sites. Additionally, you should take advantage of all the security features offered by your trading platforms. All top exchanges offer 2-factor authentication, which adds a layer of user verification upon login and withdrawal request, ensuring that your account remains secure even if your password falls into the wrong hands.

Unfortunately, some types of deception are not so simple to protect against, including ICO fraud. With a nice website, a thorough white paper and a convincing team page, intelligent scammers can swindle investors out of tens of millions of dollars.

They raise funds for a fake project without any intention of fulfilling the promises laid out in the roadmap, and once the fundraiser is concluded, they simply disappear with the money. Thanks to the anonymity of many cryptocurrencies, this is all too easy to accomplish and it's the sole responsibility of investors to avoid such traps.

Read through the white papers of all coins you invest in, verify their team members, and steer clear of any projects that make unrealistic promises.

51% ATTACKS

One kind of attack making headlines this year is actually due to a vulnerability in certain blockchain networks, and that is the infamous 51% attack. In order to understand this attack, it is first important to comprehend what makes a blockchain secure. The reason that Bitcoin's blockchain cannot be altered is that the data in the blockchain is validated by millions of participants, or "miners," scattered across the globe.

No single miner owns the majority of the network validation power, called the "hashrate," and so nobody has the power to influence or alter the information that is being validated. When a blockchain is properly distributed in this way, the information within it remains tamperproof.

The problem with smaller networks, such as that of Verge, for example, is that there are not enough validators participating in the network and so the majority share of validation power can be produced by a single party - given that they hold enough mining power to compete with the rest of the network validators.

Once they achieve the majority (51%) of the network hashrate, the blockchain is essentially theirs, and they can rewrite the data however they choose. Scammers often use this power to change the history of transactions on the network, re-routing tens of thousands of coins to their own personal wallets.

05 APPLICATIONS OF BLOCKCHAIN

"The old question 'Is it in the database?' will be replaced by 'Is it on the blockchain?'"

- William Mougayar

STRATEGIC BUSINESS VALUE OF BLOCKCHAIN

So, what is an actual blockchain?

To get into the history of it a little, "Blockchain" is the brainchild of Satoshi Nakamoto, the elusive mathematician who created Bitcoin. Simply put, a blockchain is a distributed record of information that is verified in groups, or "blocks," using a scattered computing network. By design, blockchains are incredibly secure as the information stored within them is verified by every network participant, and no single participant owns or controls the information.

The ingenious structure of a blockchain can be applied anywhere, offering advantages of accountability, efficiency and transparency.

Bitcoin was conceived in an effort to produce digital assets that could not be duplicated. The problem before the advent of Bitcoin was that all digital assets, or files, could be copied over and over again. For example, if someone sends you a PDF, you can copy that PDF and send it to your whole contact list. This was a major problem for currencies of the internet, as people could spend them multiple times and there was no accountability for the total supply.

The Bitcoin network, secured by a blockchain, requires every validator of the network, or "miner," to agree on the location of every Bitcoin (BTC) token. In order to move tokens, a BTC sender must wait for the network to verify the legitimacy of the transaction and provide a consensus, which is then stored forever in the blockchain.

Though the original blockchain was only created to solve the double- spend conundrum of digital currencies, the ingenious structure of a blockchain can be applied anywhere, offering advantages of accountability, efficiency and transparency. Let's take a look at some industries that could benefit from the new technology.

IDENTITY MANAGEMENT

A static blockchain of identity-related information can become essential for businesses, governments, and individuals alike. For the individual, it provides unprecedented ID security. Everywhere we go, we are constantly being asked to share personal information to gain entry into places or access services. Any time we share a credit card, share a driver's license, passport, or social security number, we put ourselves at risk of identity theft.

Uploading our personal information onto a blockchain would ensure security and immutability, giving each person a self-sovereign identity. When your information is verified on a blockchain, you no longer need to provide sensitive information to prove your identity. Your legal name and birthday would be enough to locate and confirm your record.

A government-issued blockchain identity, which is already being used in Estonia, offers a safe and un-hackable civil registry. This grants the government knowledge of exactly how many citizens it has, who they are, and where they came from. It can also offer citizens a digital "vote" associated with their blockchain identity that would forever be connected to them. With a voting system verified by a blockchain, a government can ensure there is no voting fraud in any election, and that all votes are cast by legal citizens.

HUMAN RESOURCES

In a business context, an employer could replace traditional ID cards with a blockchain-based identification system. This would enhance the security of office buildings with restricted access and improve the security of sensitive documents which are only accessible to certain employees.

DYNAMIC DIGITAL REGISTRIES

A dynamic digital registry, such as the one used for the Bitcoin network, is constantly updated by the participants on that network as assets that are registered on it are exchanged or moved around. This type of network can be used for anything from real estate buying and selling to managing the supply chain of, say, rice or corn or diamonds.

With this technology, any asset, such as a house, car, or piece of artwork can "tokenized," for digitally enabled fractional ownership, and digitally represented on a blockchain. Once an asset is tokenized, its ownership (by any number of participants), history, and whereabouts can be forever traced on the distributed ledger. This means that you can't lose the title to the car, or have the deed to a piece of property disappear in a natural catastrophe or through an act of mismanagement.

REAL ESTATE

In the case of real estate, this is especially interesting. An apartment complex could be tokenized and sold in millions of pieces to an unlimited number of buyers, including the tenants of that actual building, and each buyer could collect dividends proportional to the piece of the apartment that they own. In this way, owning equity in real estate no longer requires tens of thousands of dollars up front, and the doors are open for anyone to become a real estate investor with just a small amount of money to invest. The same concept can be applied to fine art and other expensive commodities that have been traditionally only offered to the elite.

MEDICAL SUPPLY CHAIN

A dynamic registry can also provide efficiency and peace of mind in supply chain management. A business can easily track the location and status of every item in their inventory in real-time from production to distribution as it is continuously updated on a blockchain.

Additionally, since blockchain ledgers are often publicly auditable unlike private databases, a consumer can track the production of any products they buy, from food to drugs. In this way, someone with food allergies can have peace of mind that their Oreos never came near a tree nut, and they can ensure the safety and legitimacy of the Epi-pens they buy.

SMART CONTRACTS

Blockchains also facilitate autonomous, self-executing arrangements called smart contracts. Smart contracts are a written set of conditions that complete an action once all conditions are met. They require no human interaction beyond creation and they are examinable by anyone. Their transparency and self-governing nature guarantee that they will function exactly as written, without the need for outside verification or enforcement. This makes them an ideal infrastructure for processes such as escrow services, initial coin offerings, lotteries and insurance claims.

With the current government- run lottery system, there is no way to know for certain how much money has been raised, how many participants are involved, if the winner selection is fair, and if the money actually ever goes to anyone.

Escrow services built on smart contracts can negate any need for disputes when the two parties involved agree on a set of terms. For example, Party A deposits funds into a digital escrow account, and upon completion of a service by Party B, the funds are then released to Party B. If Party B fails to meet the terms of the agreement, the funds are released back to Party A. With all terms and actions recorded and authenticated by the escrow blockchain, both parties can be sure that the process will carry out as expected without the fallible input of a human.

Likewise, smart contract-enabled lotteries and contests can certify that the contest is fair and legitimate. With the current government- run lottery system, there is no way to know for certain how much money has been raised, how many participants are involved, if the winner selection is fair, and if the money actually ever goes to anyone. With a smart contract, participants can see the terms of the lottery and prove that a winner is chosen at random and they are paid as promised.

Ultimately, the advantage of blockchain is the elimination of the need for the trust of another party, and a blockchain can be applied to any operation that needs additional transparency and independent corroboration.

06

ALGORITHMS EXPLAINED

"The purpose of a consensus algorithm is to allow for the secure updating of a state according to some specific rules... meaning that no single or colluding set of actors, can take up the majority, even if they have a fairly large amount of capital."

- **Vitalik Buterin**

ALGORITHMICALLY SPEAKING

If the opening quote to this chapter is a bit confusing, here is the entire quote, verbatim, below. If you have seen any Youtube videos of Vitalik Buterin talking about blockchain, then you know he is extraordinarily intelligent and specific in his phrasing. Don't let this throw you off, though. His interest in algorithmically supporting different ways for people to engage a system that is designed to not have any centralized authority is pretty profound. It's like if you tried to code the actual language of democracy. How would you incentivize people to vote, or engage? How would you keep the power of the whole from falling into the hands of a select few? The types of algorithms that we dive into in this chapter, illustrate different ways that this type of democratic engagement can be supported within the blockchain.

"The purpose of a consensus algorithm, in general, is to allow for the secure updating of a state according to some specific state transition rules, where the right to perform the state transitions is distributed among some economic set. An economic set is a set of users which can be given the right to collectively perform transitions via some algorithm, and the important property that the economic set used for consensus needs to have is that it must be securely decentralized – meaning that no single actor, or colluding set of actors, can take up the majority of the set, even if the actor has a fairly large amount of capital and financial incentive." -Vitalik Buterin

CONSENSUS ALGORITHMS

A consensus algorithm is a term used to describe a protocol that is enables us to realize a consensus, or an agreement, among distributed systems. Blockchain consensus algorithms are used to ensure that blocks of data are legitimate and contain correct data. They also act as a security system, preventing any single antagonist from confusing the network and creating illegitimate "forks" (where a single blockchain splits into two or more separate blockchains).

The consensus algorithm, while being one of the most overlooked components of any prosperous cryptocurrency, is arguably the most important key to the long-term success and security of a blockchain. One of the first problems that must be solved in order to create a functional distributed network is known as the Byzantine Generals' Problem.

BYZANTINE FAULT TOLERANCE

If a system has Byzantine Fault Tolerance (BFT), it can remain stable and functional in the event of a failure caused by the Byzantine Generals' Problem. Often, malfunctioning components of a distributed network can give false or conflicting data to different parts of the system, which causes discrepancies that can only be resolved by achieving a universal consensus. This problem was originally described in a 1982 paper from Robert Shostak, Leslie Lamport, and Marshall Pease titled "The Byzantine Generals' Problem," using the subsequent metaphor:

Several Byzantine generals, each directing their respective portion of the Byzantine army have surrounded a town. They need to decide whether or not they are going to siege the town, but they must decide in unison to avoid an uncoordinated attack, which could end in tragedy. Because of their distance from one another, messengers must deliver notes between the generals, and their reliability is not guaranteed. To add further complication, a mischievous or corrupt general could intentionally prevent the group from reaching a consensus.

In order to overcome the challenges described above, a solution is needed that will ensure the following: all cooperative generals agree upon the same plan of action—to retreat in unison or attack in unison; and that a minority of traitors cannot sway the majority vote in any undesirable way. Though the problem may sound simple, an algebraic evaluation shows that it requires at least $3n + 1$ cooperative generals to overcome the issues created by n uncooperative generals. Simply put, a lone renegade can sabotage the vote of two cooperative generals. More than two-thirds of the generals must cooperate in order to achieve a "correct" outcome.

The problem that they face is finding an agreement on a single plan of action among dispersed components. It is an issue of consensus and a consensus protocol is necessary to solve it.

A consensus protocol must be capable of finding agreements on single values of data despite possibilities of malfunctioning components in the network. In other words, a consensus algorithm must be fault-tolerant. Byzantine Failures are errors caused by misinformation being spread to the network (e.g. a node generating random data while posing as a genuine contributor). A network that can resist these instances without losing stability or consistency is Byzantine Fault Tolerant.

Byzantine Failures are errors caused by misinformation being spread to the network.

The first major breakthrough in solving the Byzantine Generals' Problem for distributed data processing was presented by Satoshi Nakamoto in an e-mail back in November of 2008. He announced that "the proof-of-work chain is a solution to the Byzantine Generals' Problem," and the Bitcoin consensus algorithm was born.

PROOF OF WORK

Proof of Work (PoW) was the original consensus algorithm created for blockchain technology. It is currently employed by Bitcoin, Ethereum, Litecoin, Zcash, and may crypto-enthusiasts' favorite meme-coin, Dogecoin. In a PoW network, miners (computers) dedicate enormous amounts of computer power toward solving difficult, often redundant mathematical problems in order to achieve a consensus with one another and produce blocks of validated data. Because of its long running track record of securing the Bitcoin blockchain, PoW is considered by many to be the most secure consensus protocol, though it is not without drawbacks.

As the Bitcoin network grows in scale and popularity, the demand on electricity can become a dangerous threat to the health of our environment. At present, the network already consumes as much energy as the entire country of Denmark. This consumption will only multiply as more people get involved in Bitcoin mining.

Other consensus algorithms have been conceived to solve the power consumption issue, and though they are only in their infancy compared to PoW, some are already showing promise.

PROOF OF STAKE

Proof-of-Stake (PoS) is similar to PoW, though no mining is required. Instead, minters (not miners) validate the blocks by staking their tokens. The more tokens a minter stakes, the more validating power they hold within the network. If the blockchain were to fork, or split, minters will spend tokens to vote for support of one of the forked blockchains. If most validators voted on the "correct" chain, then those who voted for the less popular chain would lose their stake in the correct one.

The problem with Proof-of-Stake is that nothing is really at stake for the minters. Since they don't have overhead expenses of hardware and electricity like miners do, minters can vote for both sides of every fork that occurs with no consequences, leading to many unnecessary forks which damage a blockchain's credibility over time.

DELEGATED PROOF OF STAKE

Delegated Proof-of-Stake (DPoS) was developed by computer scientist and EOS creator Daniel Larimer. In a DPoS network, a small group of validators is elected by the token holders to make choices on their behalf. Having only a few validators allows them to coordinate with each other and create the most efficient schedule for block producing. If a delegate is not performing up to par, they can be voted out of their position and replaced by a better candidate. In DPoS, the miners collaborate with each other instead of competing for rewards like they would in a PoW or PoS system. Though the partial centralization is not popular in the cryptocurrency community, it is very efficient and EOS, which employs DPoS, is on track to be the first blockchain with a block time of one second or less. For comparison, Bitcoin's block time is 10 minutes.

PROOF OF AUTHORITY

Proof-of-Authority (PoA) is a protocol in which data is validated by pre-approved users only. They act as the administrators of the system, and they are not usually appointed by any democratic process. PoA offers a high throughput, but its centralization only lends itself to private networks. Blockchain users expect trustless systems, and PoA does not provide this.

PROOF OF WEIGHT

Proof-of-Weight (PoWeight) is a customizable protocol that allows users to have influence in the network based on a number of weighted values. In PoS, the weight is determined by the number of tokens staked. In PoWeight, it can be something such as clout within a network, or the amount of InterPlanetary File System (IPFS) data stored on a user's device.

07

"Blockchain doesn't just enable social movements, blockchain IS a social movement."

- Herb Stephens

SOCIAL IMPACT OF CRYPTOCURRENCIES

When creating the technology behind Bitcoin, Satoshi Nakamoto envisioned an efficient, peer-to-peer payment system that required no institutional involvement. Ultimately, he hoped to change the world of online payments – but the potential impact of his invention is much, much greater than that. Beyond changing payment systems or inciting wild investor frenzies, the technology at the heart of Bitcoin holds the potential to have a profound impact on the world's social sector in the 21st century.

Anything from property sales to supply chain management can benefit from the simplicity of an open cryptographic ledger.

Though the word 'blockchain' is currently most associated with various forms of digital currencies, the technology can be used to record virtually any form of electronic data in a secure and autonomous manner. Anything from property sales to supply chain management can benefit from the simplicity of an open cryptographic ledger. By using a distributed validation process for these types of exchanges, the need for third-party verification (auditors) is completely negated, saving individuals and businesses valuable time and money.

Similarly, blockchains used by governments would enable automated compliance systems and remove the need for many of the current government surveillance entities such as IRS. With incomes posted on a blockchain, the function of the IRS could be carried out with a simple autonomous contract.

Blockchain technology is only in its infancy and has yet to realize its full potential. Currently, only 0.5 percent of the world's population is using a form of blockchain, while more than 50 percent of the world's population uses the internet. As blockchains begin to show everyday use cases, their adoption is likely to explode in the same way that the internet did years ago.

PHILANTHROPY AND INTERNATIONAL AID

In a webinar for Forbes.com, Ric Shreves of Mercy Corps challenges the audience to "imagine a technology that could allow an artist to automatically donate 50 percent of royalties from a specific song to their charity of choice; that could help homeowners conserve electricity with a 'smart' refrigerator and then automatically donate the money saved to charity." These kinds of systems can be easily created and self-governed with blockchains.

In many regards, humans are wasteful. We waste energy, we waste gas, we waste water, etc. One of our biggest wasted resources is food. According to the World Food Programme, 815 million people (one in nine people in the world) go to bed hungry every night, and one in three suffers from some form of malnutrition. In contrast, the National Food and Agriculture Organization found that roughly 33 percent of food produced in the world every year -- over 1.3 billion tons -- is wasted or lost.

If all food production were accounted for on a single ledger, supply chains could become more flexible and allow for the dynamic rerouting of unused food.

As an example, if a shipment of produce to Kroger does not meet their standard of quality, a blockchain-enabled smart contract could quickly and dynamically reroute the shipment to another grocer – or to a charity – without a burdensome additional expense.

In the future, not only will blockchains allow philanthropy to become a seamless part of our daily lives, they will also increase the transparency of charitable organizations.

Blockchains can also govern the redistribution of our other most wasted resources, including energy. Historically, energy has been an expensive and environment-taxing resource to produce, with much of it still going wasted. With a simple smart contract, a family with solar panels could automatically donate or sell at discounted price their surplus energy to their grid-reliant neighbors.

In the future, not only will blockchains allow philanthropy to become a seamless part of our daily lives, they will also increase the transparency of charitable organizations. With the open and autonomous nature of blockchain smart contracts, contributors to a charity can each hold a real-time copy of the fund's ledger and verify that their contributions are being used as promised.

GOVERNANCE AND DEMOCRACY

Governments, while reluctant to embrace a decentralized currency, will likely adopt some form of blockchain-based voting to strengthen and secure their democratic processes. A blockchain system will add integrity to existing voting systems, enabling secure and anonymous voting and removing the possibility of electoral fraud -- which has been a topic of great concern in the United States.

While helping the government itself, this system will also add the benefit of trust in a time when the public trust in government is at an all-time-low.

As Bitcoin's blockchain prevents anyone from double-spending BTC tokens, a voting chain prevents any users from casting a double-vote, as well as preventing any tampering with the collected data. The votes can also be cast from anywhere in the world without compromising security, allowing someone in active military duty to participate in democratic processes without the need for an absentee ballot.

While helping the government itself, this system will also add the benefit of trust in a time when the public trust in government is at an all-time-low. Participants in a vote can watch ballots being counted in real-time on the ledger and they can be confident that the votes are real and accurately reported. With a paper ballot system, there are many points of vulnerability in which votes can be miscounted, misreported, or even edited.

If a government operated with blockchain technology behind it, issues of budget and supply mismanagement would be a thing of the past.

Aside from voting, blockchain technology can be used to replace government auditors and intermediaries entirely, saving countries millions of dollars every year. Traditionally, revenue services such as the IRS attempt to collect taxes from citizens after the transactions have already occurred, counting on intermediaries and citizens themselves to correctly report the amounts of income. If a government introduced their own cryptocurrency and issued wallets to each citizen, revenues would be recorded openly and reliably in real time on a ledger, allowing taxes and tax returns to be automatically calculated and deducted by smart contracts.

Additionally, if a government operated with blockchain technology behind it, issues of budget and supply mismanagement would be a thing of the past. According to USA Today, a recent federal spending report showed $619 billion dollars went missing from

302 different federal programs. The Department of Health and Human Services failed to report nearly $544 billion in Medicare spending, the Department of the Interior did not report any spending for almost half of its assistance programs, and the White House itself failed to report spending for any of the programs it is directly responsible for. Not to mention the Pentagon's logistics agency lost track of over $800 million earlier this year.

With the sheer amount of money and the number of programs that the government is responsible for, a blockchain is crucial for proper management. Keeping all of that data organized on a continually validated database would increase the government's efficiency exponentially, eradicate a multitude of losses, and eliminate the need for retrospective budget reporting altogether.

CONCLUSION

"Instead of putting the taxi driver out of a job, blockchain puts Uber out of a job and lets the taxi drivers work with the customer directly."

- Vitalik Buterin

The complexity of blockchain technology does not lend itself to easy comprehension, and consequently, its mass adoption will likely be a longer that enthusiasts like me are hoping for. Without being grounded in a thorough understanding of how blockchains work, opinions of the industry can be easily swayed by dramatic news pieces, which are hot one day and cold the next. Seeing headlines speculating the future Bitcoin price from $0 to $1 million, it can be easy to perceive it as an investment only for the likes of gamblers. And seeing headlines of Bitcoins being seized in FBI drug busts, it can be easy to perceive it as a tool for criminals.

But my hope is that this book has offered a better understanding of blockchains and the advantages that they provide. Armed with this insight, it becomes clear that blockchain will one day revolutionize not only finance industry, but every system that we currently rely on, from all-encompassing governmental organizations to things as small as our in-home Wi-Fi networks.

For the first time, the world has a system that allows people to escape the shackles of centralization. Nothing in our lifetimes, not even the internet itself, has held so much potential for disruption. Mega- corporations like Amazon will eventually be replaced by blockchain systems that will carry out peer-to-peer distribution networks autonomously, maximizing efficiency and reducing costs for sellers and consumers. Many finance-related jobs such as accounting will become a thing of the past as all transactions will be automatically tracked, calculated, and balanced on certified, real-time ledgers. Even government agencies themselves, such as the IRS, will no longer be needed.

Each day, systems are being developed on blockchains to heighten transparency and remove the unnecessary middlemen profiting off of the services we buy. A redistribution of wealth and power is imminent and many of the world leaders that we know today will soon see the end of their reign. It sounds theatrical, but it's already happening, and there's little that anyone can do to stop it.

To be a part of the revolution, it's critical to support budding blockchain projects by adopting their products and services, providing feedback, and spreading awareness. Educate your friends and family by talking about it with them. Get into a heated blockchain argument at Thanksgiving dinner (or just a nice discussion). I know, Grandma may still struggle with how to use her smartphone's texting feature, so this may fly over her head, but the more people who understand even the basics about blockchain technology, the sooner the negative stigma will dissipate and we will see our daily lives permeated by the advantages of this technology. Not to mention, the sooner you adopt it yourself, the more likely you are to build significant wealth from the eventual growth and acceptance of digital money and blockchain. Anyone who does not get involved in this wave of innovation, even by simply understanding it, will surely be left behind.

ABOUT THE AUTHOR

Monika is an artist, entrepreneur and speaker working at the nexus of fintech, real estate and social impact. She has founded businesses in the real estate, technology, fine arts, education, and hospitality sectors. Through these endeavors, she has brought a social impact ethos and a tangible, sustainable investment of over a million dollars to one of the poorest regions in the United States, southern New Mexico.

Monika's expertise showcases how the convergence of new technologies will enable the consumer of the future to be the driver in nearly every vertical of the new, post-blockchain economy. Her passion for engaging marginalized sectors of the value chain shines through in all of her endeavors. From discussing new marketplace entry points, to describing how consumer and worker interests will be reflected in new market movements, Monika enthusiastically illuminates how blockchain technology is set to disrupt how we think of consumers, creators, and drivers of value in the global economy.

She lives in New York City.

To learn more about the author and keep abreast of new developments, visit:
http://monikaproffitt.com/blockchain